You Need It,
I GOT IT!

You Need It, I GOT IT!

Conversations with Global Entrepreneurs
on Growing Your Audience, Visibility & Influence

A COLLABORATION PRESENTED BY:

Tieshena Davis

YOU NEED IT, I GOT IT!

Published by Purposely Created Publishing Group™

Copyright © 2017 Tieshena Davis

All rights reserved.

No part of this book may be reproduced, distributed or transmitted in any form by any means, graphics, electronics, or mechanical, including photocopy, recording, taping, or by any information storage or retrieval system, without permission in writing from the publisher, except in the case of reprints in the context of reviews, quotes, or references.

DISCLAIMER

This book is intended for informational purposes only. Users of this guide are advised to do their own due diligence when it comes to making business decisions and all information, products, and services that have been provided should be independently verified by your own qualified professionals. By reading this guide, you agree that the author is not responsible for the success or failure of your business decisions relating to any information presented in this book.

Printed in the United States of America

ISBN: 978-1-949134-45-2

Tieshena is available for speaking engagements,
book signings, and workshops.
Send your request to booking@publishyourgift.com

Special discounts are available on bulk quantity purchases by book clubs, associations and special interest groups. For details email: sales@publishyourgift.com or call (888) 949-6228.

For information logon to:
www.PublishYourGift.com

DOWNLOAD YOUR GIFT!
FREE IMPLEMENTATION PLAN WORKSHEET

READ THIS FIRST
Thank you for purchasing this book!
As a token of my appreciation, I'd like to give
you the companion tool at NO COST.

DOWNLOAD YOUR GIFT AT:
www.asktiedavis.com/goals

Table of Contents

Welcome to the Conversation! 1

Meet the Visionary Compiler
Tieshena Davis 3

Introductory Interview with the Profit Accelerator™
Allyson Byrd 5

LESSONS & GROWTH STRATEGIES
FROM GLOBAL ENTREPRENEURS

Lesson 1:   Social Impact Entrepreneurship
Katrina M. Harrell 9

Lesson 2:   Media Pitching
Maleeka T. Hollaway 17

Lesson 3:   Image & Style Consulting
Idalia "Dalia" Wilmoth 25

Lesson 4:   Platform Building
Shani E. McIlwain 31

Lesson 5:   Education Reform
Yawne Robinson 39

Lesson 6:   Grassroots Marketing
S. Monique Smith 45

Lesson 7:   Digital Marketing
Kemya L. Scott 53

Lesson 8: Strategic Management
DeAngelo McCoy 61

Lesson 9: Personal Performance
Ifedayo "Dayo" Greenway 69

Lesson 10: Special Needs Parenting
Sabrina Thomas 75

Lesson 11: Holistic Restoration
Joyce Kyles 83

Lesson 12: Business Startup
Lashana N. Williams 91

Lesson 13: Building Relationships
Tanya Barnett 97

Lesson 14: Emotional Wellness
Yah Hughes 103

Lesson 15: Life & Work Balance
Tracy E. Mitchell 111

Lesson 16: Team Building
E. Che'meen Johnson 117

I GOT IT! IMPLEMENTATION PLAN 125

We're sure you've learned a lot from these conversations. Now it's time to turn your biggest takeaways into action!

Welcome to the Conversation!

With almost 30 million entrepreneurs in the United States alone, it is easy to get lost in the shuffle, causing you to be overlooked, overworked, and overwhelmed in your business. To stand out, it is imperative for you as a business owner to foster brand sensibility and effectively market, and most importantly, follow through with the unique solutions you can offer to your ideal audience.

Compiled by Multi-Award-Winning Entrepreneur, Tieshena Davis, *You Need It, I Got It* spotlights sixteen trusted coaches, consultants, and advisors who share industry-specific lessons and strategies to teach you how to conquer common entrepreneurial challenges, tailor your passions to guarantee the betterment of your business and dominate in your niche.

Through transparent advice on tried-and-tested practices for success, this book provides an invaluable space for you to connect with global leaders in entrepreneurship and use their expertise to build on your own, making it possible for you to grow your audience, increase your visibility, and expand your influence.

Entrepreneurship is an intentional lifestyle designed and nurtured by your mindset, passion and determination to succeed. *It is your obligation as an entrepreneur to evolve*, failure is not an option.

– Tieshena Davis

Meet the Visionary Compiler

Tieshena Davis

Tieshena Davis is a multi-bestselling author, creator of the Indie Author Legacy Awards (IALA), and the founder of Purposely Created Publishing Group, an international award-winning firm specializing in author branding and development. She appears widely at professional events, teaching audiences how to leverage writing to advance their business and career goals in competitive environments.

Within the past decade, her work and contribution in the publishing industry has led her to being awarded 2017 Medical Moguls Academy *Faculty of the Year*, honored as Prince George's County Maryland *Top Forty Under 40*, and recognized by Examiner.com as 2015 *Best of the Best in Publishing*.

Tieshena's expert advice has been featured on *Fox 45, Rolling Out*, *The Huffington Post*, *Black Enterprise, Publishers Weekly, Forbes.com* and other numerous media outlets. She's a graduate of Yale University School of Management Book Publishing Executive Program, and an active member of the Independent Book Publishers Association.

To learn more, visit www.AskTieDavis.com

Do more, be more,

create more,

and oh yeah–

MAKE MORE.

–Allyson Byrd

Introductory Interview with the Profit Accelerator™

Allyson Byrd

Tieshena Davis:
I know over the past decade you've helped hundreds, if not thousands, of entrepreneurs rapidly increase their audience, visibility, and influence in various industries. As a global sales strategist and leadership expert, what do you think the biggest challenge is for new entrepreneurs?

Allyson Byrd:
The challenge for most entrepreneurs is that they are seeking monetization as their first step of success; however, they are unaware that there's a four-part prelude to ensuring the money can actually happen—not once or twice, but in a recurring process that stabilizes their cash flow, allows them to scale their business for substantial growth, and eventually, makes it possible for them to buy their way into the freedom they ultimately desire and deserve.

Understanding that, here is the four-part prelude we must abide to accelerate our results for growing our audience, visibility, and influence:

Part 1: Product or Solution Mission
What is the purpose of what you've created, and who will it most accurately serve NOW?

Part 2: Product or Solution Messaging
How are you communicating and demonstrating this solution so that others instantly perceive their need for you, it, and the promised outcome?

Part 3: Product or Solution Methodology
What is your unique value position that instantly intrigues the potential buyer to rise up, self-identify, and demand that you take them on as a client?

Part 4: Product or Solution Movement
What is your "what the hell" moment where your potential lead looks at what you're bringing to the table and asks, "Why have I never seen it like this before?"

When you have established the **mission** of your work, mastered the **messaging** and how you share it with the part of the world that needs it, further vetted its viability through the buildout of your *methodology*, and secured your relevance through a **movement** of raving fans, you, my friend, enter the world of Cuba Gooding Jr. and his famous line from the movie, *Jerry Maguire*: "SHOW ME THE MONEY!"

I love your philosophy on "The New Age of Influence." Does influence alone deem a business as successful?

If you're an entrepreneur, there are two things that matter most to your ultimate success: *customers* and *cash flow*. Without those two things, you have an idea, and likely a glorified hobby, but you don't have a business.

Introductory Interview with Allyson Byrd

Along with my four-part hack system, the lessons shared in this book are what you need to consider if you want to instantly expand your market reach in a meaningful and profitable way. *You Need It, I Got It!* creates the ideal space for any entrepreneur who's ready to do more, be more, create more, and oh yeah--MAKE MORE.

Allyson Byrd is the CEO of
Money Movers International.

To learn more, visit her website at
www.AllysonByrd.com
Connect on social media at @allysonbyrd

LESSON 1

Katrina M. Harrell

Social Impact Entrepreneurship

Katrina M. Harrell is an accountant, bestselling author, inclusion and diversity advisor, community advocate, and strategist for entrepreneurs and organizations. Katrina proudly served as an AmeriCorps VISTA for Habitat for Humanity International and is highly active within Wilmington, North Carolina, serving and working strategically with community-based organizations to develop initiatives and programs around poverty alleviation, economic development, and affordable housing.

Katrina received a bachelor of science in accounting with a minor in finance from Saint Peter's University and completed the executive program in social impact strategy from the University of Pennsylvania. After working as a corporate accountant for twelve years, in 2008, Katrina became president of KM Harrell Group, LLC, a business development firm with a focus on helping businesses and organizations sustain stronger profits while expanding impact. KMHG recently co-founded The Launch Project, an economic empowerment business training company for underserved individuals in predominately distressed communities.

To learn more, visit www.katrinamharrell.com

You Need It

As a business strategist and advisor in the economic and community development industry, I work with businesses and organizations, as well as individuals who are seeking to create a business, that create jobs within their communities.

It's important for leaders in this space to master…

Social impact entrepreneurship. As a leader, you have to be involved and be aware of what the issues are and what barriers are hindering us.

I became a key influencer by…

Spending time in the community and recognizing what the real issues are. To give a quick background, I was a corporate accountant for about twelve years. I worked for major corporations as well as many thriving small businesses. When I left the corporate world, I began consulting for small businesses, and I noticed a trend. These small business owners had created thriving businesses while creating jobs within their community, where jobs typically were scarce, and were able to employ 50 to 200 people within their community. I also noticed that some of these businesses and entrepreneurs lacked business acumen in regard to structuring a business. For five years, I worked with these small businesses to develop strategies in their operations, systems, and infrastructure.

As a direct response to my realization of what issues businesses were facing, I started my business Your Simple Bookkeeper to support small businesses that struggled with proper financial management. During that time as an entrepreneur, I paid a lot of attention to my clients, specifically to the entrepreneurs' intentions and their reasons behind starting businesses. Every one of them had this bigger goal of being able to support their community in some way. They wanted to be successful themselves so that they could provide jobs and support the success of other people. That, coupled with my same desire and wanting to know how I could best be used, steered me in the direction to study more of the community development aspect of entrepreneurship, which at the time was a relatively new concept.

For example, the practice of the business Toms Shoes is, for every pair of shoes purchased, they give a pair of shoes away to a child in need. Their business model, which is essentially "buy one get one," was one of the first mainstream businesses that made social impact entrepreneurship popular. Businesses have been giving back for years, but people were able to see this in action.

I decided to become familiar with the social impact model, which involves a company using their business to create social change for individuals. I was introduced to a program called AmeriCorps, where individuals and professionals provide one year of volunteer service to nonprofit organizations in the United States. For a year, I served with AmeriCorps and worked for a nonprofit organization that focuses on building and selling homes to low-income individuals at affordable rates. I supported them by providing capacity building services and expertise from 20 years of corporate and entrepreneurial experience.

During my time with AmeriCorps, I worked in the community and gained a new perspective. Initially, I viewed entrepreneurship solely from a business perspective, but when I served in AmeriCorps, I was able to see the need for entrepreneurship to promote community development. I saw the impact of poverty and all the different things that fuel poverty—for example, violence, low test scores, history, community racism, and gentrification. I'm a solution finder, so going through this experience made me realize I have a much bigger calling as an entrepreneur.

How can entrepreneurs grow their businesses and increase their profits while maintaining the culture of the business?

Create an operational structure. Business owners owe it to themselves to have solid infrastructures that are able to function and operate properly because businesses have the capacity and the responsibility to change the landscape of a community.

As the entrepreneur, it's important to do some soul searching: Why are you in business to begin with? Why is it so important for you to be in this particular business? What are your personal goals? What is your why? The combination of understanding yourself and understanding what motivates you to be an entrepreneur will help you design a structure within your business that supports your vision.

The biggest challenges are…

Knowing how to grow, how to stand, and how to be able to reach their goal and their dream of hiring people and further enhancing the community.

My advice to you…

Along with specifying your intentions in business, you need to have a good understanding of the needs within the community that you are doing business in. When you understand the needs of the community—who is in need of jobs and why there is a lack of jobs—and the culture of the community, then you can better understand how to hire the right people, decide which industry you should be working in, focus on what your business should be doing, and learn how to find more customers.

The key advantage to knowing what needs in the community your business can fulfill is that it brings liberation and freedom. It's wonderful if you can eat well individually, but it's even better when you can look around and see other people eating at the table with you. One of the beautiful gifts that we have as entrepreneurs, is that we get to create a new life, a new world, and a new vision not only for ourselves but for other people.

The downside to not giving back to the community in your business is that you will have a business where you're the only one who's eating at the table, and that's no fun. But even more practical than that, we have communities that continue to deteriorate. We have communities where gentrification is moving people out and crime is increasing. Poverty, accessibility to jobs, low-performing schools, incarceration—these are all connected. By not looking at your business as this bigger mandate, if you will, you will miss out on sharing your gift of entrepreneurship and helping people live better lives.

I'm here to serve you…

If you are interested in creating a successful business that can grow and operate without you, need help developing operational infrastructure or improving your current business model, and are ready to discover your ultimate why and purpose in entrepreneurship.

Let's connect!

Email: katrina@katrinamharrell.com
Twitter: @katrinamharrell #LoveLiberates

> Businesses have the capacity and the responsibility to change the landscape of a community.
>
> – Katrina M. Harrell

Social Impact Entrepreneurship

I Got It!

Write down your biggest takeaway from this lesson:

LESSON 2

Maleeka T. Hollaway

Media Pitching

Maleeka Taliha Hollaway, a native of Atlanta, Georgia, is the founder and CEO of The OfficialMaleeka Group, LLC, a boutique firm specializing in business lifestyle coaching, consulting, writing, and public relations. Maleeka is an internationally certified life and business success coach, a candid public speaker, a member of the highly esteemed Forbes Coaches Council, and two-time best-selling coauthor of *20 Beautiful Women: Volume 2* and *Release: Untold Stories About Inner Strength, Resilience, & Overcoming Challenges.*

With a devotion to mentoring and coaching people of all ages and genders in discovering how to live the life they desire, Maleeka is blossoming into one of the most inspirational and influential millennial voices of this generation. After earning a bachelor of arts in English from Alabama A&M University and a master of science in communications, she is now pursuing a doctorate in business administration with a concentration in leadership from Capella University.

To learn more, visit www.theomg.biz

You Need It

As a coach in the public relations industry, I have created a signature model on how to pitch to the media and land successful mentions and citations. I work with authors, speakers, and coaches who seek to build or establish their personal or business brands within the industry, and are looking to get more exposure and buzz about who they are and what they do, so they can reach their customers and clients, and therefore make their business and their brand grow.

To gain more visibility, it's important for entrepreneurs to…

Do your research. Know who you are targeting and know what it is they're interested in. Know what's going on in your market concerning your expertise before you try to connect with anyone. Doing your research will guarantee that you're not stuck in the dark.

What is the strategy to being featured in major media outlets?

Clients always want to know how to get to the big guns, how to reach those large publications, such as *Forbes* and *Huffington Post*, that only the elite get a mention in or get their business featured in.

In creating my game-changing strategy, I honestly just fell into it. Someone once told me that I'm a connector of people, and people flock to me because they either see I'm connected to someone or they like my energy and charisma. I play on that a lot when I'm looking to connect with a particular platform, whether it be an individual or a business, such as a digital publication. I have a lot of conversations and interactions on social media. First, I get to know the person of interest and let them know who I am. I tell them I enjoy their work, and I share my ideas on what they have done to give them another angle to look at. I make sure our connection moves past the initial communication to a point where the other person realizes how I can benefit them and how they can benefit me.

To be featured prominently in the media, start small and start local. Start with smaller publications so that you build buzz around yourself. If someone were to Google your name, they would see that you didn't just start doing coaching all of a sudden, or you didn't just launch a book today and decide you wanted to be in *Forbes* or *Huffington Post*. They will see that other people are interested in you, and visibility is all about creating that interest in what you're doing and gaining credibility. If you start small and get mentions of your business circulating within those smaller brands, when you do go to pitch to a larger brand, your background and experience make you more marketable.

The biggest challenges are…

With your mindset. Many of you 1) are unclear about how to communicate who you are or what you do and 2) have a limited mindset. For example, someone may think, "I wrote a book, but I'm not a writer. I don't know how to write. I don't know how to pitch." You have to get past that mindset of saying, "I don't know," and instead say, "Let me find out."

My advice to you…

When trying to gain more visibility, ask for help when you need it or look at what someone else is doing. For example, you can participate in webinars or attend conferences. It often takes making a financial investment and a time investment to perfect what it is you're trying to represent to clients, but just remember that "I don't know" is no longer a viable option. If you don't know, find out how to do it. If you need help pitching, go find out who is the best pitcher or reach out to your prospect and ask them what they are looking for. Or, do the research yourself. It's all about getting started and getting your feet wet. You'll never know or you'll never perfect how to pitch or how to communicate who you are if you never do those things and never get feedback. Ask someone you trust for their feedback so you can make sure you're on target. You have to get your head in the game and just go for it.

If you get rid of the "I don't know" or "I can't" mindset, you will unlock a lot of possibilities for you, which will set you up to win. Change your thoughts and decide that if you are working toward something for yourself, you will give it all you have. Another advantage is that you will know how to communicate who you are and what you do. This does involve some logistics, like training and strategizing, but more than that, it's important to be passionate about who you are and what you do. Sometimes, people don't necessarily care how you do something; they just want to know that you can do it. If you're excited about it, then naturally it's going to make people want to lend you their ear or turn your way and see what you have going on.

The downside to keeping that negative mindset is that you will stay stagnant. When you have something that you know you've been called to do, and it feels like no one is supporting you or no one is interested, it will cause you to doubt yourself and whether this path is the right one for you. You can have an amazing business or an amazing book, but if you don't get the support that you know your soul needs, your fire will burn out. That's never a good thing because you don't want to be in that place where you're second-guessing your purpose because you're not supported. It's important to get accolades because it will inspire you to be better, and to continue to outcompete yourself.

I'm here to serve you…

If you are interested in coaching and communication, need help with getting your brand the credibility it needs, and are ready to get out there to meet everyone you're supposed to meet.

> Let's connect!
> Email: maleeka@officialmaleeka.com
> Twitter: @officialmaleeka #TheOMG

It's important to be passionate about who you are and what you do.

– Maleeka T. Hollaway

Media Pitching

I Got It!

Write down your biggest takeaway from this lesson:

> Knowing your true identity is very important in building your image and personal style of dress.
>
> – Idalia "Dalia" Wilmoth

LESSON 3
Idalia "Dalia" Wilmoth
Image & Style Consulting

Idalia T. Wilmoth is an authentic advocate and researcher who considers herself a trendsetter—a person who disrupts the norm of beauty in ways that are transformational for women. As the founder of Pretty Authenticated, an aesthetics movement offering services such as stylist workshops and social events, Idalia's mission is to enhance self-determination, embrace style, and provoke success.

Idalia received her bachelor's degree with a concentration in humanities and arts and a strong background in Africana studies from Indiana University–Purdue University of Indianapolis, and she is currently a graduate student at Indiana University School of Education, where she is earning her master's degree in urban education. To help you uncover your authentic self through the lens of aesthetics, Idalia passionately speaks about authenticity in fashion, meaningful beauty, and how to determine individual style.

To learn more, visit www.PrettyAuthenticated.com

You Need It

I am a consultant in the fashion and beauty industry, and I specialize in bringing the aesthetics of dress into contemporary times, specifically in regard to black women. I work with women between the ages of eighteen and forty-five to help them find the origin of their style, their beauty, and their authenticity.

How can women find their unique and authentic style?

Many women say they don't have style and that they're "plain Janes," but every woman has style. You just have to dig deep enough. Unlike fashion, style comes from within, and my mission is to help my clients figure that out. We go all the way back to their natural characteristics from their DNA. I ask them: Who are your parents? What is your background? What was your environment growing up? Were you raised in the city or on a farm?

Then, I ask them about their influences. For example, for me, my influences were the ladies in the church. I saw the way they dressed and the way they carried themselves, and that guided my personal style. To tap into your true identity, you have to take these steps of self-reflection. You might have to go back to that little five-year-old girl who went through some trauma, or that five-year-old girl who loved flowers, to figure out exactly what your personal style is.

What is aesthetic dress?

The concept of the aesthetics of dress has been around since the 1800s, during the Victorian era, and it involves understanding the value and having a deeper appreciation for beauty in how it relates to dress, how it's valued, and how you can have a particular experience based on dress. Even though this concept has been around for some time, commonly, it only focused on white women. I want black women to understand that there are standards of beauty they can create.

An example of aesthetics of dress in the black community is when Angela Davis came out with the Afro and all black clothing. Today, we as black women can continue to be liberators in the way that we dress, and as a result, improve our self-esteem and get back to our authentic selves. I want to help place black women back into a standard of beauty of that nature.

What is the most important thing to know about building your image?

Knowing your true identity is very important in building your image and personal style of dress. A lot of times, women dress based on what's trendy. We see what's going on in the media, and we try to compete with one another. I want women to realize their true identity and self-image, so they can add value to this world.

The biggest challenge is…

A lack of confidence. Many women do not know who to turn to when it comes to fashion, style, and beauty. A lot of them have problems with trying to figure out who they are in fashion, and this can be difficult if you're comparing yourself to someone in a magazine who you may not necessarily relate to.

My advice to you…

You have to take authority! You have to get to the point within yourself where you are ready to not care about what people are talking about in society. You have to get to the point where you are sick and tired of society telling you to dress a certain way or be a certain way. You have to be ready to show up and be authentic. In order to get there, you have to dig through the closet and dig deep into yourself to figure out how to be authentic in the way you dress.

The key benefit to connecting with your authentic self is that you will bring value to your life and business. When you know who you are, you tend to serve in the space that God has given you. You know how to operate in the things that you value.

The downside of not doing this is that you're going to become a walking mannequin. I say that because mannequins are staged. They're only presented in the window for a period until someone decides to change the way they look or what they're wearing. I don't want anyone walking around as if they are not of value or as if they lack substance. You can try to fake it till you make it, but that usually doesn't work well because you're not feeling good about yourself. If you don't take the opportunity to get to know exactly who you are and what you want in life, people are going to run over you.

I'm here to serve you...

If you are interested in creating your personal style, need help with building your image to make a lasting impression, and are ready to get fashion and beauty recommendations.

Let's connect!
Email: Prettyauthenticated@gmail.com

Image & Style Consulting

I Got It!

Write down your biggest takeaway from this lesson:

LESSON 4

Shani E. McIlwain

Platform Building

Shani E. McIlwain is the founder of Practical Partners, an administrative support services agency dedicated to helping authors, speakers, and coaches with day-to-day operations. Being an author and speaker herself, Shani understands firsthand the importance of having a streamlined process to successfully operate a business.

As the host of her own Blog Talk Radio show that airs every Monday night, Shani shares love, light, and life with thousands of listeners across the country. Known for her candid personal stories, she weaves her "messy" moments of life into practical teaching moments for others.

Shani motivates her audiences with practical principles to be effective in all areas of life. Her transformative messages help people change their mindsets, shift perspective, and maximize the potential within.

For more information, visit www.practicalpartners.info

YOU NEED IT

As a platform building advisor, I help authors and coaches leverage vending events to gain more speaking opportunities. My target audience is writers who are looking for ways to grow their audience. Generally, they have less than six months of speaking experience, or maybe they have written a book or are in the process of writing a book, and they are trying to branch out into the speaking arena.

All current and aspiring authors should be…

Persistent. When I became a published writer in 2015, I wanted to use my book to leverage speaking opportunities. During my first year in this business, I focused on trying to find vending opportunities, and I went to at least four to five vending events a month. I was very strategic about what type of vending opportunity I was going to select. I researched ways to connect with my target audience and develop relationships with the decision-makers of those conferences. I created a spreadsheet of every single event that I went to, and I got laser-focused on annual events or events that had been put on multiple times because I knew that they would most likely do the event in 2016.

After participating in an event, I always sent a thank you letter to the event planner or whomever I had correlated with to get my vending table. I kept them in this funnel of information, so I added them to my blog list and to my website, and connected with them on Facebook, so we were able to develop and maintain a relationship online. About eight to nine months before their next annual conference, I would reach out to them and say, "I know that you do your annual conference. Are you looking for a speaker?" Through that experience, I realized that being persistent in finding the right events and the right relationships was a process that worked.

How can authors grow their audience and visibility?

Gaining more visibility is all about networking. You can gain speaking opportunities through networking, building relationships with people, and supporting other like-minded people who host events. A lot of times, speakers host their own events and are looking for future participating speakers. If you know someone you did a panel discussion or a workshop with, you can always return the favor and ask if they want to work together again. It's about establishing authentic relationships, with an emphasis on "authentic." Don't be fake. You have to be clear with people about your intentions and your goals.

Also, you can't give up. This goes back to what I said earlier about persistence. It took me two years to build a relationship with someone who I wanted to work with. I wanted to be on their platform, and for a while, it just wasn't the right time, but now, two years after building that relationship and cultivating that relationship, I was asked to speak.

The biggest challenge for new speakers is…

Finding the right opportunities in the right market.

My advice is…

Do your research, especially if you're new in the speaking arena. If people don't know you as a speaker, your phone is not going to ring and you will not get an offer to speak for two thousand dollars. You have to research and find smaller events and workshops. You can search on Google for conferences in the genre you want to speak in. For example, my genre is faith based, so I look for Christian conferences. Go on sites that sell tickets for conferences, like EventBrite. People put their conferences on those websites to promote them. Don't limit yourself to conferences in your local area, but look throughout the United States. This will broaden your level of opportunity so you can find your niche audience. Also, it's important to know that you can't be a speaker for every audience.

The key advantage in doing research is that it opens up more opportunity, and you will be better prepared. Not every conference or event that you end up going to will work out in your favor. I have gone through a lot of trial and error. I went to a conference that I thought was ideal for me, and in terms of profit, it was my biggest failure. But I met people who I was able to either invite on my radio show or find a way to collaborate with in a different way. Every conference that you go to or every vending opportunity that you go to, you might not necessarily come out ahead in terms of monetary success, but you will always be able to work on forming relationships, building your email lists, and making contacts and connections. Look at that as being successful too.

Another key advantage is that you will get out of your comfort zone and move into things you really like to do. As a public speaker, you love to speak, so getting those opportunities will make your business grow, and if your business is growing, hopefully your life is growing as well.

If you don't stay persistent in research and relationships, your business will be stagnant. You're not going to get speaking opportunities, and people are not going to notice you. Your platform is not going to grow, and you're not going to get recognized.

Platform Building

I'm here to serve you…

If you are interested in learning how to build your speaking platform, need help with researching and finding speaking opportunities, and are ready to add an additional stream of revenue to your business model through public speaking.

> Let's connect!
> Email: contact@practicalpartners.info
> Twitter: @Shanimcilwain #Sharingwithshani

Don't be fake.
You have to be clear
with people about
your intentions and
your goals.

– Shani E. McIlwain

Platform Building

I GOT IT!

Write down your biggest takeaway from this lesson:

_____

_____

_____

_____

_____

_____

_____

_____

_____

_____

_____

_____

_____

_____

_____

_____

_____

Understand your population and understand who is on your team.

– Yawne Robinson

LESSON 5

Yawne Robinson

Education Reform

Yawne Robinson is a passionate educator, author, educational data analyst, academic coach, founder and CEO of the literacy program Reading 4 Smiles, and advisor for The Educator Suite, LLC. Through her many roles, she strives to impact educators, parents, and most importantly, children by using her skills to make sure quality education is available for those who need it. With a passion for business and education, Yawne works with educators, leaders, and consultants in the industry to improve areas such as school culture, data impact, and building educational businesses.

A resident of Queens, New York City, Yawne loves to travel and provide service in her community. She currently serves as the second vice president of the Astoria Branch of the NAACP and is an appointed member of Community Board 1, which votes on decisions that impact the local community.

To connect, visit her website at
www.theeducatorsuite.com

YOU NEED IT

As an advisor in the education industry, I help school leaders and those who are interested in opening up educational businesses or schools to create a culture of learning and mentoring youth for academic success. I have created a philosophy for merging personal and professional development to successfully achieve goals such as analyzing data, fostering school culture, and building schools.

To attain success, leaders in education should…

Give yourself space and flexibility, and know that you cannot do it alone. When you want to be impactful to the population of children and staff that you serve, you have to be flexible and open, but also, you have to keep a clear vision of what you want to accomplish. The day-to-day struggles inside of a school can become very foggy, so clarity is necessary to bring your vision to life and to deliver the best possible school or educational business you can.

How can leaders in education create a positive and productive culture?

I have been in the education industry for about fifteen years, and I've always been on the administration end. In addition, I have served many roles in the educational sector, from admissions in operation to school management to data analysis to start up, and then, I launched my own educational business, Reading 4 Smiles. From all of my experience, I have learned that for the vision and the how-to steps to be completed, you must be organized, be clear, hire quality people, and most importantly, build solid relationships. Either you have to be a true visionary or you have to hire a person who is a visionary to be on your team.

The biggest challenge is…

Trying to serve a population of students who are either high risk, meaning high in need because of specialized services or intervention services, or students who are succeeding above measure. This stems into another challenge: How do you keep those students engaged?

My advice to you…

Creating a strategy is key. That way, you will know how to solve any mishap before it actually occurs, and you will have a plan in place. To do this, you have to understand your population and understand who is on your team. The best way to do that is to create a model that focuses on what you're trying to accomplish and what experiences you want others to have, as well as what growth is necessary, both with the staff and the students, to make a positive impact.

The key advantage of creating a strategy is that you will develop a cultural community of learners because 1) you're looking at what your staff needs in order for them to develop personally and professionally, 2) you're looking at what the students need to succeed academically and become more well-rounded, and 3) you're closing these gaps of community involvement because now you're making a connection between students, family, and educators.

If you don't have a clear plan and intention, you will stay in a spiral, feeling drained, like you've lost your edge. Your team will be unhappy, causing you to be unhappy with them and vice versa. You will not meet your overall goal for student achievement, and you won't get to see the positive results from both the students and your staff.

I'm here to serve you…

If you are interested in developing a quality school that has a high bar of success for student testing, student achievement, student work, and student goals, as well as teacher attainment and retention; need help with developing a school program model or literacy component model that works in developing your student and your team; and are ready to help those who need the help—those who want better, who need advice, who need to revamp or create structure, or who need another set of eyes on program- and goal-setting for their school or business.

Let's connect!
Email: theeducationmessiah@gmail.com
Twitter: @TheEdSuite #educatorsuite

Education Reform

I GOT IT!

Write down your biggest takeaway from this lesson:

LESSON 6

S. Monique Smith

Grassroots Marketing

S. Monique Smith is the founder of the Known As Monique Foundation, Inc., a nonprofit organization in Baltimore that offers advocacy support, education, prevention programs, and resources related to the issues of missing persons, child abduction, and human trafficking.

After spending nearly thirty-two years on earth, surviving a childhood of severe abuse, and being blessed with four children, Symbolie Monique Smith learned that she did not exist. The face of missing children everywhere, Monique is currently listed in both the national NamUs registry and the National Center of Missing and Exploited Children as a living, unidentified person, given the details of her presumed abduction and inability to unearth her true identity.

To learn more, be sure to visit
www.KnownAsMonique.org

YOU NEED IT

As an advisor in the community outreach industry, I work with advocates of social responsibility who are trying to support community efforts across many platforms such as homelessness, child abuse, sexual abuse, and human trafficking.

What's the most effective way to build an audience?

Create and leverage partnerships. If you put in the legwork to gather a network of contacts, you will gain a plethora of resources, which will support your community even further. Along with providing your services, the companies you partner with can provide different services that ultimately reach the same goal.

It's important to form relationships with individuals and businesses who share a similar platform to yours. For example, if I wanted to advocate for human trafficking, I would research organizations that deal with child abduction or missing children, connect with the right people in these businesses, take advantage of their networking opportunities, and then offer them something in return. It's about more than what a company can do for you; it's about what you can do for each other. It's about creating a win-win situation where you can give each other support, share your resources, and build on that relationship to form other partnerships. You will be able to become an advisor within your platform because you will start to build these resources and become known in your niche. It's important to put yourself in the right places with the right people who can support your cause. Remember—it's not going to always be perfect, but at least you're out there.

Is there a specific approach to initiating partnerships?

Yes, the right approach is to identify and apply. First, identify your purpose and the purpose of your potential partner. Then, apply that knowledge to your conversation with them.

For example, let's say I attend an event for human trafficking. I have identified my purpose of advocating for missing or abused children, and I have identified the connection with the event, because in a lot of cases, children who are abducted are forced into human trafficking. Now, how do I apply? I apply it in my conversations with people by seeing who I can connect with who needs my information or my resources, and vice versa.

This method can work for any networking event. Even if someone representing a specific business isn't in the same industry as I am, I ask them, "Have you exhausted your financial support this fiscal year? If not, would you like to make a contribution to my organization?" In my case, a lot of times, people know about child abuse, but they don't know the numbers or specifics. In your conversation, you can identify what your specialty is, what your needs are, how they can help you, and how you can help them in return. In addition, always let them know that their help is going to spread additional awareness and save lives. Helping gives them an opportunity to be socially engaged in what is happening in the community, which is beneficial for any business.

The biggest challenge is…

Gaining the financial support, whether it be for community engagement, resource materials, or networking materials. There are so many organizations now because becoming a nonprofit or a grassroots organization has become more accessible. Also, the economy of corporate

You Need It, I Got It!

America is taking a big hit, which means those big grants that are normally utilized or the funds that are usually given to charities are drying up. It can be very difficult for people to get that financial support.

My advice to you is…

Make your inquiry small, but make your reach large. To explain, let's say you are trying to raise twenty thousand dollars for your cause. Instead of asking one company for twenty thousand dollars, ask twenty companies for one thousand dollars. That way, you're getting a smaller amount from each company, but you're asking a bigger audience, so you're still going to meet your goal.

This method has been very successful for me. I once worked with an organization that was using a house as a safe haven for victims turned child survivors of human trafficking. To keep the house open, our goal was to raise twenty thousand dollars. It was such an emergency that I couldn't go to just one person, so I asked twenty different companies for one thousand dollars each. I shared with each company what that money was going toward, and I also gave them a small certificate. This gave them something to admire, and it was a huge success. It was a win-win. The house stayed open because we received the necessary funds, and the donating companies gained recognition that they could use to promote themselves in a positive light.

If you follow this method, you will begin to build a platform of success stories that can be leveraged into even more opportunities. You can immediately come up with another platform and potentially reach out to the companies you've worked with in the past to further support the community in new ways.

Let me use another good example: I held a contributing founder networking event where each individual could pay five hundred dollars for entry or one hundred dollars. Most of the participants paid the five hundred dollars because they would always be known as the founding contributor of my grassroots organization. I now feature their logo, brand, and their business portfolio on my website, on my Facebook page, and on my other social media profiles. I also honor them throughout the year by recognizing them for the support that they gave me.

The downside to not creating relationships and gaining funding is that lives are being lost every single day. Somebody is out there waiting for you to rescue them. Somebody is out there waiting for you to be their next eyes, their next ears, their next move, and lives could potentially be lost. A lot of people are supporting you and cheering you on, and they've invested their time and energy and sweat equity into you. When you don't produce, and when you're not strategic in your plans for advocacy, you will lose some of your cheerleaders, your biggest fans, and your greatest supporters. Cross-networking is key.

I'm here to serve you…

If you are interested in creating a stronger social media platform; need help with marketing and campaigning; and are ready to consistently engage.

Let's connect!

Email: KnownAsMonique@yahoo.com

Twitter: @knownasmonique #lookup

> Form relationships with individuals and businesses who share a similar platform to yours.
>
> – S. Monique Smith

Grassroots Marketing

I GOT IT!

Write down your biggest takeaway from this lesson:

LESSON 7

Kemya L. Scott
Digital Marketing

Kemya L. Scott, marketing and social media strategist for small businesses, teaches her clients how to build a digital presence, increase revenue, and create a more successful business. Known simply as "Miss Kemya," she uses a results-focused "how to" approach in implementing simple, customized strategies so clients enjoy tangible results quickly and easily.

Miss Kemya leads each client through the social media terrain with a strategy to build engagement and drive results. She integrates traditional offline marketing tactics with the latest digital media solutions to define a customized marketing strategy that builds awareness, increases engagement, and ultimately converts leads into clients.

Contact Miss Kemya today at
www.marketingsparkler.com

YOU NEED IT

As a consultant in the small business marketing industry, I help my clients instantly expand their reach through digital marketing. My target audience is small businesses and solopreneurs, specifically people who are doing almost everything by themselves, whether they are making the coffee, buying the office supplies, setting up sales funnels, or creating their own email marketing campaigns. I work with those clients who primarily are responsible for doing everything themselves.

The beauty of digital marketing is…

It levels the playing field. Anybody can do it, and you don't have to spend a lot of money to do it. You just have to do it strategically and craft a plan so that you, as a small business owner or solopreneur, can maximize your online marketing in business.

Digital marketing gives you the ability to compete with anyone. It doesn't matter what niche you are in, and it doesn't necessarily matter what your budget is. What matters is your tenacity and your determination to use these available tools to get the biggest bang for your buck. If you position your brand properly, you can compete with major players.

How can small businesses and solopreneurs use social media to gain clients?

Marketing strategy is my passion, and with the influx of social media platforms, I added digital marketing to my repertoire to include social media. In creating a digital marketing strategy, I assess the business and figure out who the players are in that niche and what people are doing in terms of using online marketing to build their brands, whether they are using their social media pages or blogging; whether they are using Google ads or Facebook ads. Based off what these major players are doing, I craft a strategy for my client so that they can really compete.

Start with figuring out who and where your target audience is. Focus on what your business offers and who your ideal audience is. From there, we can reverse engineer the process to figure out which platforms to use with regard to social media. We can also determine what content to share on social media and on their websites in order to attract these ideal paying clients.

Depending on your niche, I'll research other companies and see what they are offering. I also look at my clients' current offerings. Are you offering products or services that your audience actually wants, or are you offering things that you think they want? Figure out what your audience wants and where they're looking on social media to find information about the types of products and services that you offer. You can also use these social media platforms to gauge your audience's interest and facilitate engagement.

It's important you know that you can't just post a picture on Instagram and then expect your PayPal account to blow up suddenly. That's not how social media works. Digital marketing is a process of becoming visible to the right people, communicating your expertise, and demonstrating your value. This strategy will lead people to sign up for your mailing list, follow your business on social media, and ultimately whip out a credit card or click the PayPal button to pay for your products and services.

The biggest challenges are…

Decreased reach (based on algorithms on Facebook and Instagram), decreased marketing budgets, and increased noise in the digital landscape. Years ago, there wasn't so much noise—anybody could start a blog, and rest assured, they could get some visibility. Your tweets wouldn't get so lost in time because everybody wasn't doing it. Now, because the digital landscape is so crowded, the primary challenge I'm seeing and I'm hearing is that people are having a hard time getting visibility online. Many small businesses don't know how to overcome this challenge because they are doing the same things they've always done, so you need to pivot and reevaluate your marketing strategy.

My advice to you is…

Look at what you're doing. If you're doing what you've always done, that probably is not going to work anymore. The thing with using online marketing tools is that the landscape is dynamic and ever-changing, so you have to keep up with the changes. This could mean figuring out how to optimize your website, deciding whether you need to find a partner, working with key influencers, or figuring out some type of outreach program. You may just need to be more visible. Instead of posting once a day, you may need to post five times. Instead of posting only about your product(s) or service(s), you may need to add a more value-based aspect that demonstrates your expertise. You have to focus on the key components of your business that give you a competitive edge and make you stand out among your competitors.

The key advantage to strategic digital marketing is that it affects your bottom line in a positive way—i.e., you will make more money. Because you are demonstrating your value, you will get more eyes on your content and gain more focus from your target audience. People will start seeking you out for offers and opportunities, so you don't have to constantly chase so many things. People will start knocking on your door because you are more visible, your content is optimized, you are on multiple platforms, your images are visually appealing, and your offers are laser-focused on your ideal audience.

The downside to not taking advantage of marketing on social media is that you will stay stuck right where you are, or even worse, you might experience a sharp decline in your business. Because the landscape is so dynamic, you have to keep up. If you don't, you may not be able to come back from that. If you don't make the change to be strategic and invest the time and effort to figuring out the digital marketing arena, ultimately, you risk losing your business.

I'm here to serve you…

If you are interested in using online marketing as the primary way to position your product and services, need help with digital marketing and social media management, and are ready to explode your business growth.

Let's connect!

Email: kemya@marketingsparkler.com

Twitter: @MissKemya #createlaunchprofit

Focus on the key components of your business that give you a competitive edge and make you stand out among your competitors.

– Kemya L. Scott

Digital Marketing

GOT IT!

Write down your biggest takeaway from this lesson:

LESSON 8

DeAngelo McCoy

Strategic Management

DeAngelo McCoy is an author, bacon-lover, business owner, coach, and all-around know-it-all. Having had his fair share of failures and missteps, he is no stranger to the necessity of a good action plan and strategy. DeAngelo, the author and creator of *Failure Rehab*, has learned how much a defined strategy will guide any vision into success with maximum impact. With that passion, he partners with leaders, entrepreneurs, and visionaries to help them craft and define strategic plans that sky rocket them to their next level.

DeAngelo is also the founder of Black Boy Beautiful, an organization dedicated to reminding and empowering African American men, young and old, of their uniqueness, humanity, necessity, and inner beauty.

To learn more, visit
www.deangelomccoy.com

YOU NEED IT

As a business consultant, I provide support to the entrepreneur or the leader who does too much. Many leaders and business owners, who often are what I call high-functioning creatives, have a dozen different things they want to do in their business. I have learned that these entrepreneurs *can* do it all, but there are certain steps they must take to discern what needs to be done and how to implement these actions to reach a higher level of success.

All entrepreneurs should…

Create a process. Having a process or system in place is invaluable to any business leader because it allows them to think in the full scope of their creativity. As leaders, especially those high-functioning leaders, we often move to the next idea so quickly that we don't gauge as much as we should, causing us to lose money, lose ideas, and lose resources. We want to go straight from our head to our hand, and while that is good and it might work, you have to stop and think, is it scalable? Can this work in a different market? Can I sell this? Can I license this? Strategy is necessary, and process is necessary. Process doesn't mean failure. It means that you're taking your time to make sure that whatever you put forth is the most effective, and it will help you pinpoint what's working and what's not.

What is the SQuad leadership and management model?

I have created a game-changing strategy that will help any high-functioning creative prioritize their goals and see them through. Even in creating this model, I went through a process. One day, I was evaluating myself in business today, and I was writing down the most valuable skills and services I can offer to other entrepreneurs.

The first word I wrote was **strategy**. That's the epicenter of everything I do. Then I wrote down **support**, because at the end of the day, I believe there's no one in the world who supports others like I can. The last two words I wrote down were what I create as a business strategist: **systems** and **solutions**. So we have strategy, support, systems, and solutions—four competencies that now come together to help or support a leader in whatever way possible. As a creative, I wanted to brand this model. I came up with the name "SQuad" to represent the four words that all start with *s*. (I always like to use alliteration in business practices because it helps me remember each step.)

Any problem, big or small, can be filtered through this model, and if you're able to employ or activate each of these competencies, as a result, you will have a working strategy. For example, if the problem is for you to get a car, you have to think, what's the necessary strategy? What type of support is needed in order to make this happen? What kind of system can you create, whether financial or personal, in order to make this work, and then what are the problems that have to be solved in order to be brought to an end? I believe you really can solve any problem by going through the SQuad model.

The biggest challenges for high-functioning creatives are…

1) Staying calm in stressful situations,

2) getting all your ideas out of your head and into action, and

3) following through with everything you want to do in life and business.

My advice to you…

Use the SQuad model. With this model, you can map out everything that needs to be solved so you already know what the end result is, whatever this x thing is. Break the plan down into four actions:

1) Put the strategy together.

2) Determine what support is needed.

3) Determine what systems are needed.

4) Determine the bigger picture (what needs to be solved).

Think about what future problems you may face and start thinking about those solutions now. If you understand the process, you will be aware of the minute details that come together, and you are able to problem solve on the spot. Even if something goes wrong in the process, you have probably already solved that specific issue twice or three times before it even happens. Whatever it is that you're doing, process is necessary, and you can't escape that. Understanding that will help you be more rational in your responses.

The key advantage to using this model is that it brings scalability and sustainability, and you're able to retain passion. As creatives and as business owners, we move on passion. We love to do the things we love to do, and the moment those things that we love to turn into work, then we no longer want to do them. Some people just like to work, but creators, specifically, go with the flow and with the feeling. Some people think that's a negative trait, but I think it's a very beautiful trait because it's something the world needs. We wouldn't be in the type of world we are in now if we didn't have those passionate leaders, those passionate business owners, who are doing what they love to do every day. This model gives you the freedom to be as creative as you want to be.

Strategy isn't a bad thing. You may find that the process is tedious, but the end result is your ability to think freely and strategize freely, so you can be as passionate about what you're doing today as the day you started. With the strategy in place, you are able to think without inhibition because you have this plan, this strategy, to be prepared.

The downside to not having a process in place is that you will lose out on opportunities. You will feel like you've missed your chance to do more in your business, causing you to end up stuck in something just for the sake of it. You end up twisting and turning your wheels forward five times over because there wasn't a system in place. You may have missed out on resources because you didn't put the right solutions in place. You won't get to do what you want to do without putting this strategy in place.

I'm here to serve you…

If you are interested in creating a strategy for your next product, program, or idea; need help with getting your ideas out and onto a working canvas; and are ready to do what you love and not just wake up to work every day.

Let's connect!

Email	hello@deangelomccoy.com
Twitter:	@Deangelogmccoy #nextlvlinc

> Having a process or system in place is invaluable to any business leader because it allows them to think in the full scope of their creativity.
>
> – DeAngelo McCoy

Strategic Management

I GOT IT!

Write down your biggest takeaway from this lesson:

Your adversaries will always be teaching tools rather than successful opponents.

– Ifedayo "Dayo" Greenway

LESSON 9

Ifedayo "Dayo" Greenway
Personal Performance

Ifedayo Greenway is a mother, inspirational writer, licensed minister, and motivational speaker who is passionate about impacting and changing lives. With a degree in criminal justice, Ifedayo has been a professional investigator for over nineteen years. Using the same research, analytical, and communication skills learned in both the professional and faith arena, she strategizes to create new methods of overcoming personal obstacles.

As the author of a conversational journal entitled *Help! My Spirit Is Overwhelmed with Hurt* and the anthology *Empowered to Become More*, Ifedayo writes for the heart that's mangled with pain, and speaks with the hopes of connecting with people's issues and being the empowering moment that pushes them to persevere. Committed to transparency and relatability, Ifedayo uses her journey, real-life challenges, and practical experiences to influence and strengthen others, encouraging them to find their authentic voice, manage difficulties, and continue to intentionally pursue goals.

To learn more, visit www.igandmore.com

YOU NEED IT

As an empowerment coach in the personal performance industry, I help women change their perspective on pain by understanding how adversaries and obstacles are strategically placed in their life to use as motivational tools. My audience consists of people who are struggling with pain and are stuck in a place of being overwhelmed from dealing with so many issues at one time.

A key lesson I share about success is…

How to leverage pain as a pathway and as momentum to move forward. This means that your adversaries will always be teaching tools rather than successful opponents.

How did you grow your influence?

By being vulnerable and sharing my relatable story. I went through a lot of different issues in my life that left me in a dark, depressed place. I was overwhelmed with the pain that I was dealing with. I had gone through a divorce, I had gone through many personal things, including with my children, and I was going through some things in church. I was consumed by this overwhelming feeling and I had nowhere to go. I asked myself, where do I turn when the pain gets to be overwhelming? What do I do with all of this? What do I do with the emotions that I'm feeling? How do I move past this place that was designed to take me out?

When I came to this crossroad, I realized I had to change my perspective. If I didn't start to see things differently, I was going to be set up for a life filled with hatred toward other people. I was going to become a victim of my circumstances rather than use my circumstances as learning experiences.

What process is necessary for overcoming pain?

You have to create a plan. Not everybody's plan is going to be the same, and you have to establish a plan that is tailored to you, whether it involves baby steps or larger steps. And as long as you have a plan in place and you're following that plan, it becomes easier to come out of anything that you're going through, and it's easier to change your perspective on it.

My advice to you...

Create your plan to overcome adversity by following my four-step system:

1) **Identify the issue.** When you identify the issue, you can acknowledge the point of pain and therefore acknowledge your obstacle. You must acknowledge the fact that there's an adversary there, and be okay with that fact.

2) **Remove the face.** When you stop seeing things at face value, you don't necessarily take everything personally or as a personal attack. If you realize it's not something that is being done to you, you can better reflect on what lessons are to be learned.

3) **Leverage the pain.** This is when you use your pain to your maximum advantage, and begin to gain clarity on the lesson that is designed to teach you.

4) **Create a pathway.** Use what you gained from the first three steps to change your perspective and move forward into the next, better phase of your life.

By following this system, you will be able to continue and foster this forward movement and momentum. You will be able to process what's happening in your life instead of ignore it. If you don't do the work to move forward, you will stay stuck. You will stay a victim. I was once at this point in my life when I was letting my thoughts go to a negative place, wondering why these situations always happened to me. If you let yourself go down that spiral, you will never get out of it. You can't let yourself be a sitting duck, even if you get tired. You've got to fight through the fatigue because that's where your victory lies.

I'm here to serve you…

If you are interested in living life to your fullest potential, need help with getting past the pain, and are ready to create forward movement.

> **Let's connect!**
> Email: ifegreenway@igandmore.com
> Twitter: @igandmore #BecomingMore

Personal Performance

I GOT IT!

Write down your biggest takeaway from this lesson:

_____
_____
_____
_____
_____
_____
_____
_____
_____
_____
_____
_____
_____
_____
_____
_____

LESSON 10

Sabrina Thomas

Special Needs Parenting

Sabrina Thomas is the mother of two sons, Shaquille and Omar, and the founder and creator of Especially Loved, a Facebook community where families with special needs can interact, connect, support, and encourage each other. Her passion for autism awareness is inspired by her son Omar, who also has cerebral palsy and an intellectual disability. She believes by raising awareness, we will enhance the lives of people with special needs now and in the future. Sabrina aims to use her experience with her son to prove that autistic people can have normal lives.

Alongside her awareness advocacy, Sabrina is working on her bachelor's degree in psychology. She is also a certified life coach and the coauthor of *Moments in Life: The Caregiver's Story*, in which she shares her story about being a caregiver to her special needs son.

To learn more, contact her at
www.sabrinatspeaks.com

YOU NEED IT

Within the parenting and family industry, I advise moms with special needs children on how to manage and balance all areas of life while raising your children.

I want moms with special needs children to know…

You are not alone. Raising a special needs child can be a lonely place, but know that there are many moms who are going through a similar situation. When I found out that my son had disabilities, I didn't have anyone in my immediate circle who had special needs children or adults. I felt alone, and I didn't have any resources. I had to figure everything out for myself. I now want to be that resource for other moms. We are on this journey together.

As an entrepreneur and mother of a special needs child, how is a balanced life attainable?

In my journey, time management has been a huge factor. I am constantly managing my time. I have a checklist for every day, and I print out checklists for the week. In my free time, I try to go over them, month by month. I write down all of my son's appointments, what needs to be done, and what doctors and therapists we're scheduled to see. You can get consumed and overwhelmed by keeping track of all the appointments that you have for your child or children, so it helps to write everything down. By being organized and detailed and writing everything down, you will be able to build a more balanced life.

Special Needs Parenting

The biggest challenges are…

The number one challenge is money. Having a special needs child can be very stressful on a family's finances. But what many people don't know is that there are many resources available, and some of those resources are free. Unfortunately, many times, you are left to figure it out for yourself like I had to. The doctor is not going to tell you, and most of the time, your child's school is not going to tell you.

Another specific challenge for parents of special needs children is acceptance. Even my immediate family and friends have to accept that this is my life right now, and I have to focus on my child first. He comes first. I can't go out with my friends or hang out with my friends like I used to because I have a responsibility to care for my child at all times. He can't be left alone, so caring for him is my priority. What I do, when I travel, where I work, what position I take, what position I don't take—everything revolves around my son because of his special needs.

My advice to you is…

If you have a child with special needs, my number one recommendation is to get support and get connected. That's what I'm all about—supporting people and getting connected with them. Like I said, when I first found out, I didn't have any connections or much support. I had to figure it out alone. There are people out there to connect with who will support you, but you have to do the work and research to get connected. There are Facebook groups and support groups all over. If you search for groups in your city, you will find that a bunch exist.

Many people tend to isolate themselves and fall into a depression. But there are people out there who feel the same way. I felt that way. I was depressed because I thought I was alone on this journey. But there are so many people out there who want to support you and who need the support too.

The advantage of being connected is that you will build a support system. When you have a child with special needs, feeling alone, rejected, and misunderstood can be traumatic. When you're connected, you're supported. You know you're not going through it alone, and that support will help you be productive for your child. If your mental state is not right, you can't take care of your child fully because you're not in a good place. So get connected with someone, whether it's your friend, your mom, your family, a member of a support group, or a combination of all of them. Also, keep in mind that a lot of special needs children don't have friends, so if you connect with people who have special needs children, your children can become friends, which benefits their well-being.

The downside of not getting support is that you will continue to feel depressed and alone, which prevents you from growing. When you're connected and supported, you get more resources. When I started out, I didn't have any connections, and I made them little by little. There are a lot of things I could have done better for my child, but at that time, I didn't know what resources I had at my disposal. The biggest downside of not searching for these resources or people to connect with is that it's a disadvantage to your child, to your family, and to yourself.

I'm here to serve you…

If you are interested in getting support, being connected, and learning about additional resources; need help with socializing and overcoming social challenges; and are ready to take your child to another level.

> Let's connect!
> Email: especiallyloved@gmail.com
> Twitter: @bre4specialneeds #EspeciallyLoved

Being organized and writing everything down will help you build a more balanced life.

– Sabrina Thomas

Special Needs Parenting

I GOT IT!

Write down your biggest takeaway from this lesson:

LESSON 11

Joyce Kyles

Holistic Restoration

Joyce L. Kyles is an award-winning, nationally credentialed speaker, entrepreneur, domestic and sexual violence advocate, and the executive director of Walking Into A New Life, Inc., an organization with the mission of promoting community engagement and sharing tangible resources for individuals affected by domestic violence. She also advocates for male perspectives, support, and inclusion of issues related to violence against women through her Men Against Domestic Violence initiatives.

Known for her transparent and passionate approach, she combines more than twenty years of real-life experiences with practical applications and professional training. To further her advocacy, she wrote a bestselling book, *Restoring the Whole in My Soul*, and hosts an online radio show, "Boots on the Ground," which addresses the intersections of domestic violence and other social points of interest around the country.

Joyce is currently married to Jason Kyles and has three beautiful children from a previous marriage.

To learn more, visit www.joycekyles.com

YOU NEED IT

As a consultant in the personal development industry, I teach people the importance of transparency to successfully overcome adversity and transform their story into a solution. My target audience is primarily women, but I work with anyone who is in need of support and services as it relates to transitioning.

To anyone who reads this chapter...

Always be yourself, be transparent, be open, and be honest. If you are suffering in your personal or professional life, do not be afraid to ask for assistance. Once you allow yourself to be transparent about your experiences, it will give people an opportunity to get to know you, allowing them to be honest and forthcoming about their situations and allowing you to develop personal and professional relationships with people.

How can we use personal barriers to increase our influence?

I began helping others with holistic restoration as a result of my experiences with domestic violence and sexual assault. In 2008, I made a conscious decision to leave my abuser. At the time, I had three children with me at home, in a city where I had no immediate family. I was ashamed of my experiences, and I finally understood that what I was experiencing was spilling over onto my children. I reflected on my life and realized that I didn't have the support of my family that I needed. In part, this was because I didn't share my experiences. I had lost everything: my home, my car, and my job. Personally and professionally, I was at one of my lowest points, but I had my family to consider. I had to look at my life and figure out what direction to go in.

I didn't fit the stereotypical description of a person who is transitioning out of abuse. Typically, people think of what a person's physical scars look like. For me, it was everything but physical. My transition began with realizing that I needed to make a change for myself and for my children. I realized that I needed to be honest with myself, and that is what I tell my clients as well. Self-reflection is extremely hard to do at times, especially when you're going through things, but I always say that the first step—acknowledging that you need help—is the hardest one, and once you have established that, you can overcome anything.

The biggest challenges are...

A lack of self-confidence and self-esteem. Often, people feel that they can't achieve their goals, and some of them are just not sure what it is they want to do. The most common challenges are understanding your purpose and then being comfortable with the process of living your purpose.

My advice to you...

To begin the process of self-reflection, take inventory of what you need, what you want, and what you desire, and then seek out individuals who are willing to work with you in a nonjudgmental environment. Be open to suggestions and constructive criticism. Recognize that whatever you're going through, whatever your adversity is, it is a journey and a process. Whether it's professional or personal, it didn't happen overnight. It happened over time, so it's important to understand that it takes just as much time, if not more, to get over those adversities.

If you become comfortable with yourself and your self-discovery, you will be able to project that information onto other people. The more you do it, the more comfortable you become and the more aware you are of who you are and what it is that you want to accomplish.

Ask for help and be honest with yourself and with the individuals who you have chosen to discuss your personal and professional goals and aspirations with. Put your pride aside and stop worrying about judgment from other people. A lot of times, what we think a person thinks of us is not what they think, but it's how we view ourselves. I always encourage individuals to just ask.

The key advantage for your business as well as your life is the self-confidence that it brings. Once you've overcome those fears and you start seeing the results of your asking, it gives you a certain ownership of your business. It gives you ownership of your personal life. It gives you a different, more positive perspective. Even the energy that you project onto others is enhanced. Once you've made that commitment to ask and then take the instruction that's given to you, you will reap the benefits in your business as well as in your personal life. Furthermore, you will give individuals you come in contact with more confidence in you because they will see what you're projecting, and they will want to emulate what you're doing. They will want to feel, look, and behave the way that you do.

The biggest downside, of course, is not living your life to its fullest potential. Often, we allow self-fear, self-doubt, and the perception of others to affect how we feel about ourselves. We're listening to people who are not in the place where they need to be or should be, so we have to think about where we're getting our information. Who are we listening to?

Holistic Restoration

To this day, I can become a little uncomfortable or unsure of myself, because as confident as I am in what I do and who I am, I still come across new challenges. I have to stop and think about who I'm inviting into my circle. Are they adding value to my life? Are they helping to advance me? What's the profit? Am I giving them what they need? If it's not mutually beneficial, professionally or personally, then we may need to consider parting ways. Another downside is holding on to people and things we don't need or want, but we may feel obligated to be attached to them.

You must learn how to let go of those things and people you don't need because once you let those things go, you leave yourself open to receive what it is that you are intended to have in this life.

I'm here to serve you…

If you are interested in becoming your best and holistic self, personally and professionally; need help with diving into personal development, overcoming adversity, establishing and maintaining self-esteem and self-worth, and transitioning from a place of awareness into a place of action and holistic restoration; and are ready to serve in the capacity that is customized to suit you and your specific wants, needs, and desires for your professional and personal life.

Let's connect!

Email: joyce@joycekyles.com

Twitter: @joycekyles #solutionspeaker

Be open to suggestions and constructive criticism.

– Joyce Kyles

Holistic Restoration

I GOT IT!

Write down your biggest takeaway from this lesson:

Be realistic about your time commitment and what's going on in your life.

– Lashana N. Williams

LESSON 12

Lashana N. Williams

Business Startup

Lashana N. Williams, author of *The Stranger Within: One Woman's Journey to Self-Love*, and CEO of Women's Journey 2 Success, LLC, is a certified career and life coach. After successfully climbing the corporate ladder from temporary employee to finance executive, Lashana served as a mentor to numerous professionals at varying levels, provided business solutions to several entrepreneurial ventures, and created a formal mentor program for a top Fortune 500 company.

As a success navigator, Lashana is committed to helping you discover your "career fit"—the career that is aligned with your passions and purpose—by offering premier programs and services to help you go from *surviving* (going to work every day counting down the minutes/hours until Friday) to *thriving* (feeling fulfilled, being passionate about your career, and having a sense of purpose).

To learn more about her programs, products, and events, visit www.LashanaCoaches.com

YOU NEED IT

As a consultant in the career development industry, I guide female parallelpreneurs through my seven-step process in personal and professional development to reach that next level of fulfillment. My target audience is women aged thirty-five to forty-five who are working full-time but are ready to launch their purpose-driven business or project, whatever that may be. I give them the tools and tips that they need to successfully do that.

It's important for female parallelpreneurs to…

Discover your purpose-driven profession, whether that be a career in corporate America or whether that be a business. You work so hard every day, forty hours a week (maybe even more), and it saddens me that you are working so much and not even enjoying what you do. Our lives are too short for that, so we need to take the time to truly discover and uncover what that purpose-driven, or custom-fit, profession is so that you are waking up every day as if it was a Friday, not a Monday.

Through my experience in business and helping others, I started to notice a common thread: success and happiness starts with you. Discovering your purpose-driven profession requires a lot of self-assessment. To take you from where you are right now to where you want to be, you have to look at your mindset and make sure it's aligned properly with your goals and plan of action.

How can parallelpreneurs manage their time for greater work-life balance?

Because you are parallelpreneurs, your biggest challenge is time management. How do you balance all of it and have a full-time job? To get a grasp on this, there are a lot of mind shifts that you have to go through because it's different than either focusing fully on your career or focusing fully on your business.

You have to be realistic about your time commitment and what's going on in your life. You have to focus on what is needed and also the resources that you have available to you at that moment. Based on those areas, you can better discern how much time you need to focus on a certain aspect to achieve this goal. It's important to understand that some of the things you want to do take time. Often, you're not going to be able to launch something in two days. But it will happen if you set realistic goals. This will also prevent you from getting depleted or frustrated in the process.

My advice to you is…

Get a system that works, whether you use your cell phone, write it down in a planner, create a calendar, what have you. Get a system that works for you so that you can prioritize your day, set your goals and tasks, and stay on a schedule. It is imperative for you as a parallelpreneur to not only carve out time but also to be strategic about the task that you tackle during that time. If you prioritize accordingly, you will maximize your time, and at the end of the week, you will have achieved your goals.

If you achieve your goals, it takes away some of the stress and frustration that some of us have when we try to do everything. Many of us are such overachievers, so we want everything to be perfect, and we get down on ourselves. But when we do that, we don't accomplish those goals, and we don't get to do everything.

Time management helps us be more realistic about the time that we have, which is one of the most valuable resources we have. If you don't put a plan in place to manage your time, it will be harder for you to finish the task at hand, and you will suffer from burnout. I've been there, and it's not a fun place to be. You feel frustrated, depleted, and like you want to quit.

I'm here to serve you…

If you are interested in making every day a Friday and discovering your custom-fit profession—the one that is aligned to your passion and purpose; need help with taking control and becoming the master of your career; and are ready to reach financial freedom and build a legacy for you and your family.

> Let's connect!
> Email: lashanacoaches@gmail.com
> Twitter: @Lashanacoaches #parallelpreneur

Business Startup

I GOT IT!

Write down your biggest takeaway from this lesson:

Use transparency to crush your competition.

– Tanya Barnett

LESSON 13

Tanya Barnett

Building Relationships

Tanya Barnett is an energetic speaker, author, and the Real Wife Coach. The award-winning author of *Being a Wife Just Got Real: Things I Wish I Knew Before I Said, "I Do,"* Tanya founded the Real Wife Movement™ to equip single and married women with tools for creating strong relationships, marriages, and families.

Through her talk show, *The Tanya Barnett Show*, Tanya provides impactful information to empower women to live life to their fullest potential in their relationships and in their businesses. She's been featured in media outlets such as *The Tom Joyner Morning Show*, NAACP, Congressional Black Caucus, *Huffington Post*, *Rolling Out* magazine, and more.

Tanya is also the founder of Forever Free Books, a mobile literacy nonprofit that delivers free books and story time to low-income children in their neighborhoods and schools. Tanya and her husband, Don, have been married for eighteen years and have three awesome kids.

To learn more, visit her website at
www.realwifemovement.com

YOU NEED IT

As a coach in the relationship building industry, I work with African American females who love their husbands, yet hate being married. These are women in their thirties or early forties, whose kids are on their way out the door, and they are ready to put the love back into their marriage.

I want women entrepreneurs to know...

In order to produce the outcome you desire in life and in business, it is all about changing your mindset and your behavior. Your relationships, including your marriage, are never as bad as you think, and you can use those experiences to learn and grow. You can take strategies that you talk about or develop in your personal life and use them in your business relationships as well.

As an entrepreneur, for a long time, I saw people as superior to me. I thought they were better than me because they had more experience or they made more money or they had a larger social media following. I had to change the way I thought about myself and the way I presented myself. I had to learn to see myself as an expert alongside other people, regardless of what my social media following was or how much money I had in the bank. Once I changed my mindset about my positioning in the marketplace, I saw my business take off, doors open, and connections and relationships form. Because I viewed myself and my business in a different light, other people were able to see me that way too.

What characteristics are most important in business?

Transparency is key. When I wrote my book, *Being a Wife Just Got Real*, I found that a lot of the women who were buying it saw themselves in my book. Women connected with me because I shared my struggle, my pain, and the bad stuff that nobody wants to talk about. I put all of that out there and created a dialogue around it, which gave women the freedom to then share with me where they were in life. They wanted my help in knowing how I went from a point of struggling in my marriage to now having a loving marriage eighteen years later. Through that experience, I realized that transparency is so important in reaching your audience and growing your business. You can use transparency to crush your competition.

Another important characteristic is patience. To get your business from where you are now to where you want to be is a process. It takes patience and faith, just like in a marriage. If you don't take the time to cultivate that marriage or relationship, or work on solving a problem you have in your business, you may be forcing something to happen sooner than it should—and this could have negative effects on your professional and personal life.

My advice to you…

Make time for a lot of personal reflection and a lot of prayer. Reflect on what role you play in each aspect of your life and see what you can do to make a change. It's so important to take your eyes off the other person and focus on yourself, because when you do so, you're more inclined to change and have the outcome you desire.

That's what I had to do. I had to work on myself and I had to get counseling. I don't think counseling is a dirty word, and it's very important for the self-reflection part of the process. Many African American women are called to be strong for everybody in every situation, whether it involves work, school, home, husband, or children. We have to be strong mentally, and sometimes we need extra help to keep it together.

A key advantage to taking the time to self-reflect is that you will have peace, you will have joy, and you will be able to function. Alcohol consumption among professional women has risen in the last couple of years because of the stress of the job, marriage, and children, so it appears as if more people are seeking peace through external outlets, whether it's food or alcohol or sex. It's important to find a healthy outlet. I know that once I worked on myself and got counseling, I started having peace in my marriage, peace with my children, and peace within myself.

The downside to not making a change in how you see yourself is being depressed. I was depressed, I was overweight, I was jealous, I was angry, I was bitter all the time. There are so many things that can trickle out of control if we don't solve these issues that we have, and many of these issues are not talked about in our community. Not talking about them leads to further stress and keeps you from solving the issue.

I'm here to serve you…

If you are interested in having healthy, holistic relationships in your marriage and business, need help with communicating more effectively with your spouse and your audience, and are ready to have the outreach you've always wanted.

Let's connect!

Email: Tanya@realwifemovement.com
Twitter: @realwifecoach #realwifemovement

Building Relationships

I GOT IT!

Write down your biggest takeaway from this lesson:

_____
_____
_____
_____
_____
_____
_____
_____
_____
_____
_____
_____
_____
_____
_____

LESSON 14

Yah Hughes

Emotional Wellness

Yahshikiah "Yah" Hughes is a mentor, an author, and the founder of Made for Purpose, a community organization that partners with women to provide emotional wellness, self-love, and motivation; and BRAVE Beauties, a female teen mentoring program that helps young ladies ages thirteen to seventeen with self-esteem, confidence, personal development, and life skills. With more than ten years of experience as a leadership trainer, educator, and faith-based preacher, Yah combines her leadership skills, counseling degree, and high-energy messages to equip people for greatness.

Awarded the 2017 Unsung Hero Award from the Delaware Chapter of National Urban League Young Professionals and the 2015 recipient of Delaware's 40 Most Influential People Under 40, Yah spends her time giving back to women's shelters, volunteering at Dover High, and mentoring teen girls in Kent County.

To learn more, visit
www.madeforpurpose.org

YOU NEED IT

As a coach in the emotional wellness industry, I teach women my transformative technique of being transparent, journaling, and confronting issues. My target audience is women who are thriving professionally, but personally, they keep finding themselves going through the same cycles of fear, abandonment, doubt, and rejection. These women are doing well from an outsider's perspective, but they've masked what has happened to them in their past, and they've masked the pain that comes from those experiences. Through my coaching, I help women who have the desire to get up, but they don't know how to get out of that painful place they've been stuck in.

I want all women to know…

Self-development is the key to every area of your life. You cannot do anything else without looking inside yourself and finding the best version of yourself. Give you a try. Give you a shot so that you can thrive in every area of your life. Dispel that myth that wholeness is not attainable for everyone. Many people think wholeness is only possible for those people who have access to better things, but it's available to everyone. It's not something for which you have to have a lot of money, or ask permission to have, and it's not something that you stumble upon. Wholeness is attainable, but you have to work at it every single day.

Why is journaling an effective tool for personal and professional growth?

We all need an outlet, some way of dealing with our emotions, and the best way to do that is to journal and self-reflect, so we can write about what we feel and what we've been through. You cannot conquer what you don't confront. By being transparent about what has happened to you and writing or talking through it, you can move forward.

While I was going through issues of getting out of my emotional pit, a place that was daunting for me, I began the process of writing out my feelings. The biggest question for me at the time was, why do people who are supposed to love me not love me? I would write that down over and over, and then write down what I felt afterward. That began my journey in therapy, and I continued to use journaling as a soothing technique to release everything I was going through. Through that process, I found out I had feelings I didn't even know were there, and I was able to reflect on how I was dealing with my issues from one day to the next.

Many people ask me how I was able to overcome my pain, and that, combined with my master's degree in community counseling, is how I got started in this industry. So many people climb out of that pit, but they don't reach back and teach other people how to do the same thing.

The biggest challenge is…

Allowing fear to drive everything that you do. You want something more, but you may not know how to get it, so you're scared to go after it. You have these amazing dreams and goals, but the thought behind starting those goals and getting to the next place scares you because of all the emotional baggage you have.

My advice to you is…

You have to work through your issues. No longer can you sweep them under the rug. No longer can you put them aside. You have to take off the mask. You have to be the major part of your own rescue. You have to look on the inside to work through your pain. And you can't go halfway through the process. Sometimes, we get to a certain point in the emotional wellness process, and we feel it's too hard because we don't want to confront or relive that pain—so we stop. But you have to continue, you have to take inventory of what's going on, and you have to confront it.

Healing is cute—you can have the best clothes, the best shoes, the best job—but if you're not healed, it makes you ugly because you're not the best version of yourself. To get to that place, you have to keep breaking it down and revisiting everything that has happened to you.

The key advantage to self-development is that you get to walk in a space and a place unapologetically. You will no longer base your decisions on your fear, your doubts, your pain, or seeds that were planted in your mind. You will get to look around and see that you are in a better place because you chose to be there. You will make decisions for you, not your pain. Your pain will no longer hold you on a puppet string, and you will wake up in the life you desired, not because someone said you couldn't or because something happened to you, but because you made every step to be where you are today.

The downside to not working through your issues is that you won't get to live the life you desire, the life you create for yourself. You will live a life based on all the negative voices in your head, the seeds of doubt, the despair of being a victim, a statistic. You will be in the same place you desired to get out of—that emotional pit. You will go through life numb. And we already know what that feels like, so why not give something else a try? Why stay in an emotional prison after the security guard has given you the keys to get out?

I'm here to serve you…

If you are interested in finding your best self, need help with getting out of the cycle of fear and pain, and are ready to get up and confront all of your "its" to take back everything that belongs to you.

> ### Let's Connect!
> Email: yah@madeforpurpose.org
> Twitter: @Yahhughes8 #madeforpurpose

You cannot conquer what you don't confront.

– Yah Hughes

Emotional Wellness

I GOT IT!

Write down your biggest takeaway from this lesson:

_____

_____

_____

_____

_____

_____

_____

_____

_____

_____

_____

_____

_____

_____

_____

LESSON 15
Tracy E. Mitchell
Life & Work Balance

Tracy E. Mitchell is an empowerment speaker and certified life coach who resides in Atlanta, Georgia. Tracy has a diverse background in nursing, personal development, coaching, mentoring, and creative writing. Tracy is the author of *Sonkissed: The ABCs for Blessed Success* and founder of "TeeMitchellSpeaks," a personal blog and website dedicated to empowering women to create and discover the hidden value in everything they possess—skills, talents, abilities, experiences, and weaknesses.

With a passion for speaking about life, biblical principles, health and wellness, and purpose, Tracy strives to enrich women physically, mentally, spiritually, and emotionally, resulting in healing and wholeness. In her free time, Tracy enjoys traveling, shopping, music, and spending time with family.

To learn more, visit www.teemitchellspeaks.com

YOU NEED IT

As a personal development coach, I teach women how to intentionally manage their time and resources to avoid quick burnout. My audience is women who are between the ages of thirty-five and fifty, and who juggle multiple roles on a day-to-day basis. Of course, many of these women are very busy and they often become overwhelmed, which can lead them to becoming stressed and sick.

It's important for women in business to learn…

To put themselves first! Women in business must learn the necessary principles of maximizing their day, their overall life fulfillment, and their influence. This involves learning how to purge and remove unproductive activities from their daily schedule, and replace them with things that will produce real results.

The biggest challenges are…

1) Balancing your time, your schedules, your priorities, and your lives in general, 2) identifying toxic people, places, and things that need to be removed from your lives, and 3) purifying or cleansing the necessary people or things to be able to reach that next level.

My advice to you…

Develop a personalized strategy. The process is going to be unique for each person—based on your personality, your responsibilities, your level of drive, and your level of commitment—but everyone must learn the unique strategies and techniques to allow maximum potential. You can start doing this by learning how to use a set process and learning how to reorganize your life so that you're removing the things that are hindering you. It's not an easy process, but you have to be willing to go through it in order to get to a new place. That process of developing strategies and maintaining self-discipline is important in ensuring that positive habits become long-term habits, and then become second nature, which will allow maximum success and influence.

If you are able to overcome your challenges with life balance, you will gain peace of mind and peace of heart. You will gain harmony and balance in every area of your life—physically, mentally, emotionally, spiritually, relationally. You will be able to live at your peak, your best place in life. And once you are at your peak, you are in the best place to serve and help others.

The downside to not creating and following a process is that you can lead yourself and others to harm, stress, and depression. All of these negative toxic thoughts, words, and emotions can overwhelm and overtake us, and potentially lead to death.

I'm here to serve you…

If you are interested in maximizing your productivity, need help with balancing your time, resources, and priorities, and are ready to move from procrastination to productivity.

Let's connect!

Email: tracymitchell504@yahoo.com

Twitter: @Iamteemitchell #powerpurge

Self-discipline is important in ensuring that positive habits become long-term habits.

– Tracy E. Mitchell

Life & Work Balance

I GOT IT!

Write down your biggest takeaway from this lesson:

LESSON 16

E. Che'meen Johnson

Team Building

E. Che'meen Johnson is the founder of Tell It Like It T'is, where she mentors people who are ready to be honest with themselves about how to heal through the power of journaling. As an author, E. Che'meen has contributed to several anthologies, including the most recent release, *A Letter to My Abuser: Once a Victim, Forever Victorious*.

E. Che'meen graduated from Marymount College, Tarrytown, with a bachelor of science in business administration. For the past fifteen years, she has held both residential and commercial property management positions throughout New York City's five boroughs. The mother of a teenage son, CJ, and cat named Sandwich, she was born and raised in Brooklyn, New York, and is a third-generation, homegrown property owner.

For more information, visit www.Echemeen.com

YOU NEED IT

As an advisor in the organizational management industry, my ideal audience consists of anyone who is willing to be honest with themselves—totally and completely honest about who they are and where they are at any present time—so I can get to know them intimately and help them make decisions that are more beneficial to them. They may have made a lot of mistakes in the past, so I help them create and organize a framework to be in a better state of mind. This process takes time, but it's important to review the full picture of who you are, and you have to address the beautiful as well as the ugly, so you can have a full understanding of yourself. I help my clients stay focused on the collective output and outcome rather than their ego, and I teach the importance of collaboration in achieving success.

To be successful as an entrepreneur, all women should…

Know thyself and trust thyself. If you do this, you will be able to react to situations in business in a more rational way. If you know yourself well enough, you will know how to calm yourself down, when to take a step back or when to step up, and trust that what you're doing has the right motive behind it. Because sometimes, we have to be careful about whether we have the right motives. Sometimes people do things just for the accolades, or to be seen as a martyr. And some people are straight up drama queens who love gossip.

For example, if you're working with a group of women for a greater good by giving back and serving your community, you must realize that your ideas are not always going to go over so well, or others may not completely understand your vision, especially when you are working with different generations. When that happens, you may have to take a back seat and accept that you are all trying to do something good, and even if your ideas are not being accepted at that moment, you can still help with the overall goal. Instead of the shine being on you, it can be on the good that is being done. It's important to pay attention, ask questions, and be totally involved in what's going on, so you don't get caught up in your head.

How can entrepreneurs use their past experiences to grow in business?

Think about what lessons you have learned from your experiences in life. Maybe you've had experiences with heartbreak or financial difficulties, and chances are, you learned a lesson during that trial, so did you grasp the lesson and hold on to it?

Especially if you're going through the same challenges multiple times, think about why you keep ending up in that situation. Maybe you didn't understand the lesson the first time, or maybe you got the lesson but it didn't take hold, or you didn't fully grasp it or pay attention. This is the case with painful experiences as well. People say "if you don't use it, you lose it," and that also applies to time. The hurt you're feeling now may not be as impactful as the same hurt that you might have felt back when you were a teenager and you originally learned the lesson. If you experience something similar twenty years later, sometimes you need to take a pause and question yourself why it feels familiar. I have a saying: if your mind can't handle something, it puts it off on your body. Things that go on in your mind do affect your body, so be very conscious of that, and when those things are happening, pay attention.

The biggest challenge is…

Confidence. Many of you lack confidence in your decisions and whether you're making the right choices. If you don't trust someone, don't go against your instinct. Don't do something or become involved with something you're not comfortable with. It's about honoring both people. You may feel a little selfish, but if you don't feel comfortable, don't push yourself to go against what you know is right.

My advice to you is…

To have more confidence in your decisions, you have to slow down and focus on yourself. A big proponent of that is journaling. Take a minute, take that breath, write it down, and get it out, because nine times out of ten, if you write it down, you will be able to see a solution more clearly. This will help you in paying attention to yourself and your instincts. You will start to see a pattern in why you are saying yes when you should be saying no, and you will start to make more sound judgments. Things will come up from places you didn't know about, especially when you know the right questions like why am I doing this? Why did I say yes when I wanted to say no? Pay attention and take time to journal and get quiet with yourself, so you can find out what's going on with you.

If you focus on yourself, you'll become more confident in your decision and no longer be a detriment to yourself or others because you're only doing things you are truly behind. As I mentioned previously, journal and get to know yourself. Make sound judgments for yourself. Everybody may not like it, but at least you will respect yourself and make the right choice for you. And that's in all areas of life, including relationships. If you feel someone has wronged you, start making decisions and

Team Building

different choices. Try not to get too much in your head of when and why things changed. You can go back through everything that you've experienced and paint it with a different color, but what does that do to you?

By having confidence in your decision-making and by knowing what you want, you will be able to work with a greater level of integrity. You will understand that not all money is good money, and you will feel more pride in what you do because it aligns with what you believe in.

The downside to not having confidence in yourself is you will always be in your head. You will stop doubting yourself and know that even though you may not always be financially profitable, you can come away with a good conscience.

I'm here to serve you…

If you are interested in being totally and completely honest with yourself, need help with using your past experiences to learn lessons and determine how to move forward, and are ready and committed to healing, being better, and being clearer.

Let's connect!

Email: info@echemeen.com

Twitter: @Echemeen #authorondeck

Have confidence in your decision-making and knowing what you want, so you can work with a greater level of integrity.

– E. Che'meen Johnson

Team Building

I GOT IT!

Write down your biggest takeaway from this lesson:

You Need It, I Got It!

I GOT IT!
IMPLEMENTATION PLAN

LESSON #_____

Goal: _____

Objectives:

What are the (specific, measurable, attainable, realistic & time-bound) steps need to help you achieve this goal?

1. _____

2. _____

3. _____

Timeline:

What is the projected start and end date for each step listed above?

Step #1 Start date _____/_____/_____

         End Date _____/_____/_____

Step #2 Start date _____/_____/_____

         End Date _____/_____/_____

Step #3 Start date _____/_____/_____

         End Date _____/_____/_____

Strategy:

How are you going to accomplish the objectives? What's your method or approach?

1. _____

2. _____

3. _____

4. _____

5. _____

Tactics:

List the tools, finances, people, products, services, technology and other resources needed to initiate the steps, provide direction and monitor your progress.

1. _____

2. _____

3. _____

4. _____

5. _____

I GOT IT! IMPLEMENTATION PLAN

Execution:

Write out your tasks "to-do" list with expected completion dates.

☐ _____

____/____/____

☐ _____

____/____/____

☐ _____

____/____/____

☐ _____

____/____/____

☐ _____

____/____/____

☐ _____

____/____/____

☐ _____

____/____/____

☐ _____

____/____/____

Key Performance Indicators (KPIs):

How will you know if you're effectively achieving your objectives? How will you measure your progress?

1. _____

2. _____

3. _____

4. _____

5. _____

6. _____

7. _____

8. _____

9. _____

10. _____

Progress Notes:

_____

_____

_____

_____

_____

I GOT IT! IMPLEMENTATION PLAN

Outcome:

I achieved this goal

☐ Yes
☐ No

List all positive outcomes

_____

_____

_____

_____

_____

_____

_____

List all negative outcomes

_____

_____

_____

_____

_____

_____

_____

More by Tieshena Davis

BOOKS

Authorlocity™

Zero-to-Zoom

Ridiculous Success

Mommy & Me Diary

Notes to My Daughter

The Mommy & Daughter Cookbook

Surviving Shocking Situations

Think Like a Bookpreneur™

LIVE PRESENTATIONS

Book Publishing 101: What You Need to Know

Make It Buzz: Building a Brand in a Digital Era

Mastering the Art of Content Marketing

Ways to Monetize Your Book Beyond Traditional Sales

ONLINE COURSES

Author Learning Lab

The Easy Book Writing System

Revenue Domination for Authors

How to Monetize Your Facebook Group

Think Like a Bookpreneur™ Masterclass

CREATING DISTINCTIVE BOOKS WITH INTENTIONAL RESULTS

We're a collaborative group of creative masterminds with a mission to produce high-quality books to position you for monumental success in the marketplace.

Our professional team of writers, editors, designers, and marketing strategists work closely together to ensure that every detail of your book is a clear representation of the message in your writing.

Want to know more?
Write to us at info@publishyourgift.com
or call (888) 949-6228

Discover great books, exclusive offers, and more at
www.PublishYourGift.com

Connect with us on social media

@publishyourgift

www.ingramcontent.com/pod-product-compliance
Lightning Source LLC
Chambersburg PA
CBHW052148110526
44591CB00012B/1893